Anxiety's Nest

Verse from the mind of
Louis Romano

Featuring the work of Alexa Guariglia

LOUIS ROMANO

ALEXA GUARIGLIA

LOUIS ROMANO

Fish Farm
Also by Louis Romano

LOUIS ROMANO

To My Sons

Table Of Contents

LOUIS ROMANO

LOUIS ROMANO

The Queen Of The B M T

She rode the subways
From the Battery
To Pelham Bay
Sleeping with commuters
To blend in and
Wrapped in old news.
She knew real hunger
And the poverty of being alone,
And the loneliness of being impoverished.
A clean toilet, a kind conductor,
And the Horn & Hardart
Blue plate special
Were her last earthly pleasures.
When found on the 86th Street platform
The two brown shopping bags
Revealed the remnants
Of her 58 years:
Two frayed blouses
Minus buttons,
Five safety pins,
A torn and worn-out nightgown,
And a gray wrap around slip.
Two pair of seamed stockings
And a few yellowed underpants.
A pair of white socks in the package
One black shoe, one brown
Different sizes.
A can of Coke.
One dollar in change.

A smashed Clark bar.
A few crushed Camel cigarettes
And two books of matches
That read, "Thank You, Call Again."
A brown envelope stuffed with yellowed papers:
Marriage certificate
Two birth certificates
Six copies of a three-name obituary.
A half-dozen Mass cards.
A rosary
A St. Joseph's Missal,
And three subway tokens.

March 22, 1978

LOUIS ROMANO

Diary #1

I view each day through eyes that will always be young.

I feel each day with fingers that will always touch softly.

I speak to everyday with a hint of a whisper tasting new sunrays or raindrops or snowflakes as they fall.

I listen to the beats of those around me mixing all the senses until everyday becomes my day and tells death that it will come too soon for me.

May 22, 1978

Do Not Bend

The mind is a file of the past,
a machine of the present,
and a tool of the future.

It controls
the past,
present, and future
in every respect.

It's a camera
that takes eternal pictures,
and pleads,

"Photos, DO NOT BEND"

April 23, 1972

LOUIS ROMANO

Nature's Touch

The sky becomes a soft blue,
And the sun gives friendly warmth.
(Then later, a raging orange.)
Awesome.
Birds, thousands of birds
sing on morning's arrival.

Little 4 year-old kids at play
the sun still working,
gently touching their heads.

Flowers bloom, grass grows,
lovers love.
Spring is born.

Now listen carefully to the sound
of the breeze passing through
the new leaves.

That is nature's applause.

May 3, 1974

For Mrs. Halper

She filled the window
on the second floor
with her size and
her smile.
Her white, white hair,
warm eyes, and
her laugh were her
age rewards.

She knew the arena well.
She watched my father
the same way but many years before
and through a different window.
I looked up every once in a while
to check that she was still
there, still watching.

She was always there.

Guarding the arena
every day, every day.

The noises were good.
A fruit-man.
A junkman.
A candy-apple man.
A Coke truck.
A knife sharpener.
Another Coke truck.

Rock 'n' Roll music
from that new small
radio made in Japan.

Things were good.
And she watched.
Every day, every day,

Things would stay this way
forever, we thought,
we hoped.

She left the window one day.
The arena was left,
unguarded.
Nothing…
was ever the same.

June 22, 1970

LOUIS ROMANO

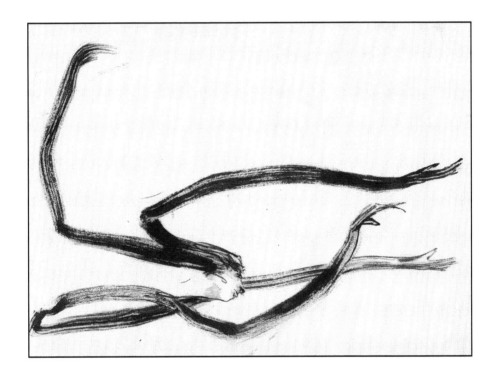

An Observation On The Grand Concourse

Miss, you have a nice baby
Very cute.
The blue oy the blue.
For the boys
For the wars.
The blue
Look...Sophie
Even the bottle
is blue.

I always had my Marvin in blue.
He loved blue.
When he left me
even his outfit was blue.
So handsome my Marvin.

Sophie, you remember!
How my Marvin loved babies!
He would always make a fuss.
Especially for the little boys.
The boys.
For the wars.

So sweetheart, when he gets the letter
do yourself a favor.
Pretend it didn't come.

And have girls darling
Have little girls.
Pray for baby girls.

They get no letter.
You should live and be well.

Come Sophie... come.

July 26, 1971

Senses

Stare deep into my eyes.
Look beyond the pleasant things
To really see.
See the buildings burning?
See them!
Feel the tension?
Feel it!
Smell the garbage?
Smell it!
Hear the red hot music?
Hear it!
Taste all of this?
Taste it!

Your heart will beat faster.
Your eyes will go wide.
Your senses will all ask for seconds.

Feel them?

May 18, 1978

Six Hells

Boldly
The mentality.
The sadistic rush.
Made the indelible mark
on humankind's complexion.

Clearly
A pox mark
on the soul of
humanity
a scar deeply imbedded
on all minds.

Openly
it memorialized
the six hells that have
scorched our
mother forever.

Treblinka
Sobibor
Belzec
Lublin
Kulmhof
Auschwitz.

March 29, 1978

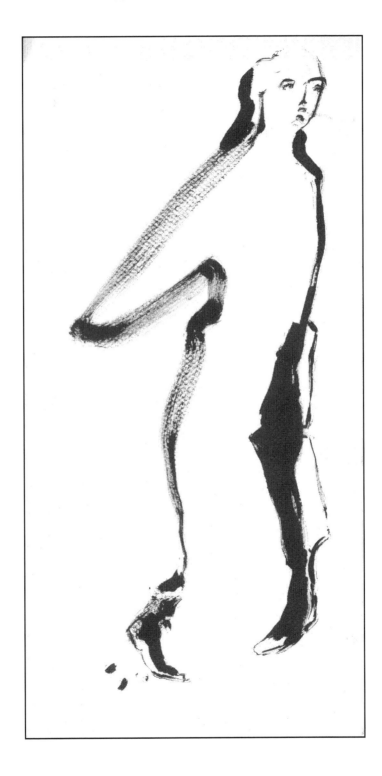

Until

Time will take its toll,
one way or another, oh yea it will.

For better or poorer
for richer or worse
until the spirit
is forced from the body
with eternal divorce.

Everything will seem
silly then,
when time takes its toll.

In due time.

In due time.

April 12, 1978

Rhythm

Let me see you
Smile wide
And see your eyes
Glisten in the
Moonlight just before
You close them.

Let me touch
Your lips and
Feel your warm
Sweetness.

Let me touch my skin
To yours
And know
All the things
About you
That I never knew.

Let me smell
The aroma
Of flowers and honey
When you appear,

And let me hear
Our hearts beating
Together
To the rhythm
Love.

LOUIS ROMANO

47th Street
(An outsider's view of the diamond district)

Hello Morris!
How are ya Sidney!
Honking.
A nice Jewish tush!
The nodding of heads
in passing recognition.
Cigar smell.
Big black bags
Silver, gold, gems.
8% that's all 8%.
Watches.
A Rolls, an armored car.
Hats, any kind, every kind.
Curls...
even on a few women.
Beards of all kinds and colors.
The young men rush around
looking for experience.
The old men move slowly
because of it.
The rain beads up on umbrellas
and long black coats.

It stops nothing.

LOUIS ROMANO

LOUIS ROMANO

And So...

Ricardo was shot under the chin at seven o'clock in the morning just two months after returning from three years in Viet Nam. Drugs or some other foolishness. At first I thought, *Why would he be awake so early?* Not surprised at his murder, but I could not understand *why, with nothing to look forward to, would he be out of his apartment so early in the morning?* I can't imagine that my response to the murder of someone I once knew would be to consider what his schedule was like. Anyway, he was 24.

March 25, 1976

LOUIS ROMANO

All, Or Nothing At All

While some follow
the words of the Bible
and others the Koran or
the Bhagavad Gita
and others the stars,
the sun, the moon,
Hari Krishna, Sun Myung Moon,
Hubbard, Buddha,
a television evangelist...

I will follow the
words of the
sacred recordings
of Frank Sinatra.

Nice and easy.

February 3, 1978

LOUIS ROMANO

Grammar Lesson 88

You' All
Y' All
All of you
Individually
Microscopically
Y'all
Are still
One
The singular
Plurally
Y'all
Becomes
Y'all
Follow?

December 15, 1978

LOUIS ROMANO

LOUIS ROMANO

A Token Of Affection

Come with me
on a subway ride.
We'll transfer
at 125th Street
and go way down
to places with
strange names
and meet people
with strange names
and eat strangely
named foods.
We can take a taxi
to a nameless club
dance to nameless
music played by
a no-name group,
and drink a
label-less scotch.
We'll ride the subway
back in wee hours,
and I'll remember
your name
if you promise
to please remember mine.

February 19, 1978

LOUIS ROMANO

A Night Out

Beer from a battle,
Nicotine and smoke,
Quick remarks
Un-cute waitresses
In dive diners
A few great pairs
Of breasts,
Pukey feelings,
Camphor blocks.
Looking for a mirror
And regretting
That one was found.
Watching some silly people
And coveting a cute ass.
Peeing between cars,
Speech slurred
By a thick tongue,
Hoping that these
Nights
will soon be memories
Not readily recalled.

March 26, 1978

LOUIS ROMANO

Once Again

Spring!
And nice again.
A solitary moth,
Earlier than the
Others, dive-bombs
A light bulb.

Once again
Love!
And nice again.
An unloved lover
Searches for
A reason
For loving.

Once again
Life!
And nice again
Dive-bombing
Light bulbs
Seems to
Be all that
Ever happens
In the early days
Of spring

March 17, 1978

LOUIS ROMANO

Call It Home
(A poem for Luis Morales)

He came into this
new world.
Not like in the
old days,
with a mule-team,
but in a U-haul,
with his family.
He didn't feel at home
in this plaster and lead
world.
He didn't feel at home,
until that fantastic
moment
when he played
A Latin record and once again
smelled the sweetness
of little oranges.

April 23, 1977

LOUIS ROMANO

Compelled

My mind forces my eyes
To see things
They shouldn't
Just so it has
Something to remember.
Even more,
It forces my eyes
To look
For things
They shouldn't,
Just to be able
To say
I told you so
When the tears come.

April 12, 1977

LOUIS ROMANO

Flashbacks

I once saw
This truck
Moving without
A driver
And took a picture
Of an old couple;
The man did not
Show.
He later died.
I saw two dogs
Fucking.
And thought they
Were stuck together
With glue.
I saw a woman
Crash her body
To the concrete
From five stories.

All that I could ever figure out
Was how the glue
Got all over those
Two poor dogs.

April 10, 1977

30,000 Feet And Falling

Free falling onto the
earth,
tumbling head over heels.
My thoughts are only of
landing,
knowing the sudden stop
kills.
But, there is that shred
of hope,
that keeps a smile on my
face.
When the smoke from the fall clears,
you can see me with a crushed
skull…
Or See me standing on one foot
giving an obscene gesture,
to the gathered crowd.

It's all in the way
the coin is tossed.

April 26, 1977

LOUIS ROMANO

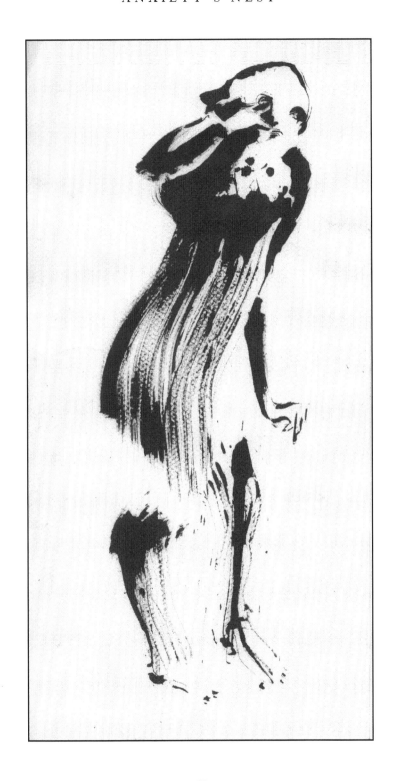

Another Story

I once found a pocket primer
of life.
It explained why life
is the beginning of death.
Why things happen in their order.
There was even a chapter on
dos and don'ts.
What one should do
for life to be what it is
for those who are always happy.
It went from the rush of sperm
to the full flooding of formaldehyde
with everything in between.
Covering happiness sorrow loneliness
and so on. And on.
My life was perfect so long as
I followed this book.
One day, so long ago,
I looked for it to tell me how to love.
It couldn't.
As I watched it burn
I understood the lessons.
And started to live;
And started to really live
And live, enjoying it all.
But love? Another story.
And so on…and on.

April 5, 1977

At Forty-Seven, Defeated

The Thunderbird wine
that was his
all-expense-paid trip to
the 4th St. Mission
a Bellevue ward
the Bellevue Morgue and
potter's field,
respectfully.

What a ride.

July 22, 1978

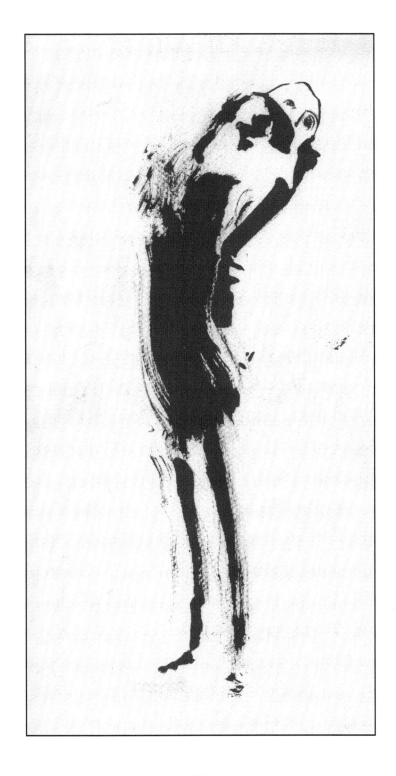

LOUIS ROMANO

Pass The Lemon Oil Please

A paper plate
wet with olive oil,
empty soda cans
full ashtrays,
and dust resembling
tumbleweed,
circle stains, greasy chips,
playing cards from a solitaire game,
and a paper cup
with the smell
of spoiled milk.

These remains of today
like pieces of days past
have dulled the surface
of the coffee table.

November 6, 1977

LOUIS ROMANO

Given A Choice, I'd Not Choose

Given a choice
I'd take a black man's life
over an Anglo's life

Given a choice
I'd live in Harlem
rather than Scarsdale

Given a choice
I'd have Converse sneakers
over wing-tipped shoes,

Given a choice
I'd read *Ebony*
over the *Wall Street Journal*

Given a choice
I'd rather live life,
than be chased by it.

Given a choice
being me,
neither Black
nor sad-assed and
pasty-faced white
Is a marvelous
alternative.

LOUIS ROMANO

LOUIS ROMANO

I Wonder How People Would Act
If They Didn't Have Hands

Hey whitey,
Get your hands off from
My body fore
I lay this
Bat upside yo' head.

Hey spook,
Walk away with
Your hands high
Otherwise I'll shoot
Ya black ass away.

Lookit bro
Hand me what's in
Your pockets before
I cut you, man.

Hey Rican
Take your skinny
Hand out a ya
Pockets and dey
Better be empty.

Put yo hands against the wall.
Get your hands off me, man.
Hand that cash across the
Counter old man.
Don't hand me that shit.

November 24, 1977

Waste

It was over
Something stupid,
—dope, money, a girl—
And as his father
Looked
On the pizza shop floor
And saw the blood
That ran through his
Veins for seventeen years
Spilled in black-red puddles,
his only thoughts
were of the years ahead,
seeing the past vision of his baby boy
covered in blood,
cluttered with sorrow.
The years of loving
building, molding
all destroyed
In a moment.
All wasted
On a stupid fight
In a damned pizza shop.
As he walked away,
He took a final glimpse

Of the picture burned
Into his mind
And began to weep
For the picture of
His son
As it should have been

July 22, 1978

Wait

When you wait for a jack
The queens and tens come.
Wait for a bus,
A taxi comes.
For a taxi, a bus.
For a queen or ten?
A Jack.
For a cop…a criminal.
Wait for a connection,
A cop comes.
Wait for a check to come
You'll get a bill.
Wait for love?
You guessed it baby.

April 6, 1977

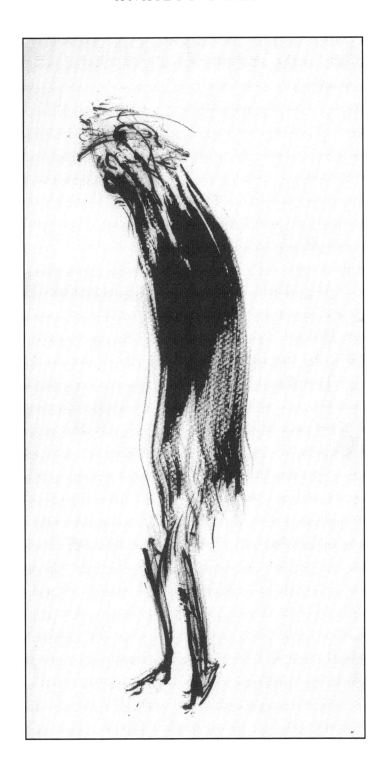

LOUIS ROMANO

The Dead

Say nothing but good of the dead.
Respect has been earned
By those who have died.
They have lived their lives
And closed their lids
To learn what no one alive knows.

We bow our heads
To death,
To the opening of doors,
Into the vast unknown,
And new beginnings.

Our respect should not be
Out of fear.

Say what you will about the living
Say nothing but good of the dead.

August 13, 1972

LOUIS ROMANO

There Is A Boat...

Leaving for the
Land that time
Has forgotten.
You can board
For very little.
Little enough.
It makes one stop
In case your mind
Changes your desires.
If you're sure
And continue the trip,
You enter a world
That was.
Search for yourself
As you were.
Change nothing.

Exactly how little
Is the fare?

All your tomorrows.

All ashore
Who's going
Ashore.

April 21, 1977

Closing Shop

Now!
If only I knew then
Look…look now.
I am closing today,
After 30 years, good years.
They stand out here,
Drinking, spitting, filthy.
Ah, once in a while
Someone still buys a cake, but…
Who had to know Spanish?
We spoke English.
It was safe,
Yeah and sort of funny
Chasing those kids,
Me with my bad feet.
Safe? Who knew killings?
Last year,
Two doors down,
The grocery man's son
Sixteen years old,
Ah, who wants to
Remember.
So now I close.
For good.
At least I stayed
'til the end.
Look, grown men
Standing out there
All day long

Drinking...
No jobs...
No money...
Nothing...
Don't stare.
Some kind
Of crazy store
Will open here
And nobody
Will
Remember

LOUIS ROMANO

Until

I've been in a building
Caesar himself would play in,
And touched the marble cut by
Michelangelo, and saw the ceiling.
I've walked down the aisle
Walked by innumerable Popes,
And saw the last supper and Mona
As Da Vinci saw them.
I touched relics of saints
And read markings of sinners.
Heard Verdi, read Dante.
I peed on cobblestones
Placed two thousand years ago,
And drank aged wines
That tasted more like
Two-thousand-year-old pee.

I've stood in awe
Of the great New York buildings,
In silence at the great statue,
And in reverence at the general's tombs.
I've seen great concerts
In the park.
Shopped on 5th,
Dined on 6th,
And danced on 1st.
And I savored the excitement
Life has to offer.

Wrapped up in the ribbon
Of life's extreme beauty.
I saw that beauty in man.
Sensing just some of what life

Should be, and wondering
At the accomplishments of the past.

Life was shining more brightly
Than any star,
And it seemed the perfect gift,
Until
Until my memory took me back
To the time, when I was five,
when I asked
An old man
to explain the green numbers
tattooed on his arm..

December 15, 1978

Marks

In the 8th grade,
My first 15 tests came back
With the following marks:
45 F see me.
You can do better
Have this signed
Careless
    D
      F
        42
           53
             26
               40
                 Sloppy
                     Incomplete
F = STUDY
Copy over 100 times.
0
So I said to myself
"Self, at this rate I
Could make a very
Successful failure."

Luckily,
One 73
Saved my life.

April 9, 1972

The Growths Of Man

I feel sorry for you because of the corns and bunions you have growing on your brain and the cobwebs that have formed around your delicate areas.

A cerebral enema might do the trick in bringing you back to humanity. After that, a good dusting of the webs and a hot bath will set the stage for your personal development. If the corns, bunions, and webs return, consider them fatal.

July 4, 1978

LOUIS ROMANO

The Prayer

The street was filthy.
Even more than he was.
He lived among the stench,
The rats, and an occasional starving dog.
Skin and bones,
He tried—oh, how he tried.
He knew there was a better life,
This was the torture.
He knew something, or someone
Could help, he hoped anyway.
He hoped, never prayed, dreamed.
The more he tried, the more he failed.
Hopes and dreams grew.
Try…try…try.
Try to clean the street
Kill the rats, feed the dogs,
Clean himself.
When he tried to clean the street
It became more filthy.
When he killed one rat
Fifty took its place.
To approach a dog with a scrap
Was impossible,
They fled
At the sight of him.
Hopes and dreams grew more.

Then one cold night
An immaculate man
Was standing
In the midst of the rubble.
The rats fled.

His presence cleaned the street
Of the garbage that covered
The cobblestones.
In an instant he was gone.
Leaving a gleaming white box.
Were his hopes and dreams answered?
The tortured man approached
The box, as if he was expecting it.
When he touched it,
When he put his hand to the long-awaited answer
The box fell apart into a pile of soot
And dirt.
The street became even more filthy.
The rats returned by the thousands.
But one stray dog came and sat
Next to the sobbing man,
And began to lick his face.
His hopes and dreams were answered.
He knelt in prayer.

November 12, 1974

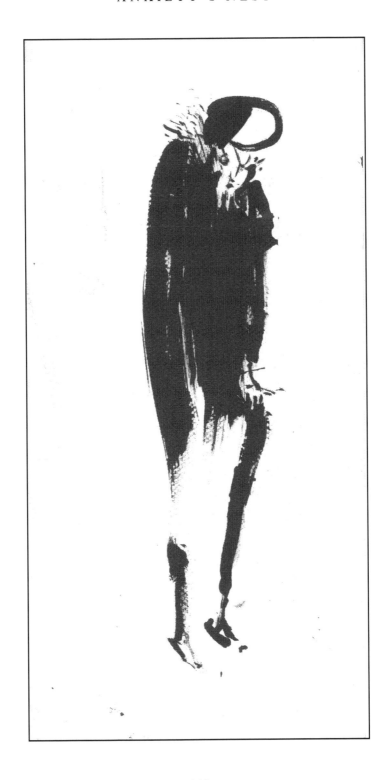

Humming

The Humming seems to
Possess the entire body,
And fill the darkness
With unknown consciousness
The eyes cannot open to
Find the humming or see light.
Motionless, timeless, still.
The mind is aware but
Does not relay its message;
No dreams or flashes,
No sound only humming.
No feelings, no joy.
No tears, no smiles,
Only humming and darkness.

August 4, 1972

Real Food

Emotions too,
Must eat.
The meat and potatoes
Are love,
Touching, the salad,
And desserts
Are soft kisses.
Tender smiles
And gentle laughter
Taste and nourish
Like milk.

Set a table,
hunger
No more.

March 26, 1978

LOUIS ROMANO

Needles And Pins

It's very
Hard to get
Close to a
Cactus.
Those little
Stickers say
"Stay away…
Or else."
It's still worth
Nurturing.
Feeding, sunning
Understand
It. Listen.
Watch, wait.
And when
The flower
Blooms, it
Says
"Come closer…
Please?"
But it
Still sticks you…

What a prick!

January 29, 1978

The Friendly Skies

My fear of flying is not
To be confused with any fear
Of dying.
What scares me the most
Is getting sick all over my
Pin-striped suit.
Falling from 30,000 feet
Can make a stomach do some
Awful things.
Then there is the underwear.

Let's not go there.

January 29, 1978

LOUIS ROMANO

One Day

On one of those
Important days
I traveled from
A newer world
To the old,
And realized little
Changes because
Of new suits
On little boys
And new white shoes
On little girls.

Just in time.

April 10, 1977 (Easter)

Out Of Heart, Out Of Soul

The heart beats fast,
the soul stays alive, aware,
vibrant, also beating.
Listen!
The rapid beating, then pounding,
makes the spirit visible,
(as feelings have matter) only for a moment which is enough...
for a lifetime.

December 12, 1978

LOUIS ROMANO

Tar Days 57-67

Sunflower and pumpkin
Seeds in red boxes,
Two-cent Coke bottles
And the bigger one
That brought the
Indian's head.
Nickel-and-diming
Ourselves in a momentary
World of twangy music
And streety street games.
Off-the-curb, skully, salluhgy,
Kick the box, the can,
Hot beans and butter, Asses up,
Nucks,
Johnny-on-the pony
Broken bones were worn
Like generals' medals.
Stickstooppaddlecurbpunch-
Foothandoffthewallballdays,
And more days,
Spent in smelly hallways
Pitching those Coke bottle coins
Hoping to win the prize
Of a big, salted pretzel
That would last ten years,
The duration of our
Tar days.
Ring-a-leveo games
That lasted the decade

LOUIS ROMANO

And spread from one block
To miles and miles
Or until Halloween chalk
Invited the frigid winds

That forced us inside
And brought cocoa to lips
That spent hours kissing
In those same hallways.
Sun returned the ball days.
Hitting fungos until the Spalding split,
Gobbling food not to miss
A trick or chick,
Always running, laughing,
Forever acting out
The game.

LOUIS ROMANO

LOUIS ROMANO

Where Does Hate Live?

The Jew bastard
hang him, kill him
they yelled.
Then the officials came in a different
time and place
wearing brown shirts
or black shirts
and would have
carried the riot
to its bloody finale.
But this time
They wore blue.
The time was 1957 and the place
could have been anywhere.
Hatred, you see,
does not have
its own
clothing.

April 13, 1978

LOUIS ROMANO

That Mile

The distance was one mile.
I walked in the rain, the cold,
and sometimes, even when the puddles
were as solid as the ground.

I couldn't stick out my arm
and point my thumb towards the sky;
I wanted to prove to myself that I could do something without
asking for help

And faces I remember
would stop and drive me there without my
having to use the digit…
Without my even asking for their help

They were nice and I thanked them sincerely,
but what troubled me more than anything
is, when my thumb is finally out of my pocket,
why does no one stop.

November 9, 1972

LOUIS ROMANO

Life...Simply Nine Boxes

The game hasn't started yet.
Sides were picked,
Coin tossed.
Chalk, a broom stick, sneakers.
A Spalding.
Ready.
The players take the field.
Home and second
Are manhole covers,
And the scoreboard
Awaits its markings
To tell the final story,
When all nine are full.

The game is over.
Rain will wash
The scoreboard away
And cool the burning
Black field.
Some have won.
Some have lost.
They all remember,

Even though
The chalk is gone.
They all await
The filling of
The nine boxes.

May 5, 1977

LOUIS ROMANO

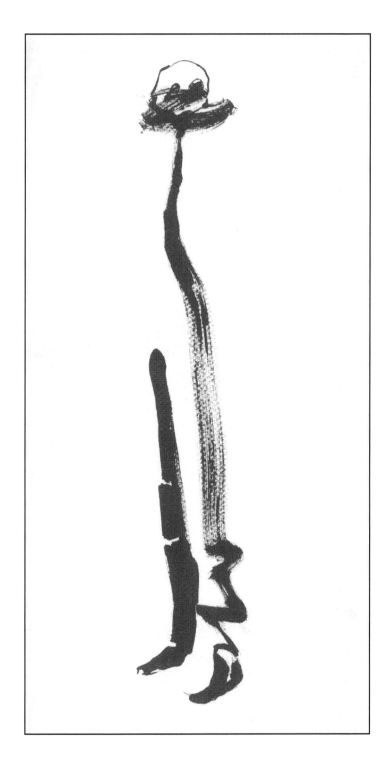

LOUIS ROMANO

Memento Of A Summer Day

The ladies
With chronic cellulite
Glance over
The darkened muscle men
With absurd fantasy.

Children, wide eyed
Chasing the surf
With colored plastic buckets
As if
There was an ocean shortage.

Varicose veins,
Bulging muscles,
Reddened skin,

Sandy bologna sandwiches,
Green flies,
Warm water,
Sea shells,
And the people,

Crammed close together:
Iron bits
Pulled to
Nature's magnet.

July 22, 1979

LOUIS ROMANO

Memories Again

Good
Memories
Are
Simply
Trances
One
Goes
Into
For
Safety's
Sake.

July 29, 1978

LOUIS ROMANO

More Stickball

Ten years
Separated Stickball
On smoldering
Asphalt.
From sipping Galliano
In the Park of Princes.
Then… I realized
How much better
The park would have been
Had I started
A stickball game.

May 23, 1978

LOUIS ROMANO

LOUIS ROMANO

Some people go after fame and fortune. Some people attain it, and the rush is still not enough. Others get the consolation prize on *Wheel of Fortune*...this is their brush with fame, their lasting memory of notoriety.

This is quite enough.

LOUIS ROMANO

The Gladiators Of The Projects

Together,
They would call
For me.
Five or six at once.
All in Chuck Taylor
Black Cons (With white laces)
Straight eyes,
Close-cropped hair,
And gloves.
I was dressed in
Shin guards, chest protector,
Mask and spikes
walked through
The projects
To do battle in
Our coliseum.
Always a fight
For life, of sorts.
To win was,
To lose wasn't.
And in the end,
it always mattered.

The Poem That Never Was

It could have been a poem,
But you crumpled it.
It could have said something,
But you tore it from the pad.
It could have started with one line
And grown into four maybe five stanzas,
But you ended it.
Who knows? It could have even
Become…a song.
Well, you'll have to live with it.
And when you see your next poem,
You'll always wonder about the
One you crumpled and tore.
That is, if you can ever write one again.
And when you read someone else's poem
And watch it mature
And get a laugh
Or cry out of it
You'll wonder
Even more.

November 24, 1977

LOUIS ROMANO

Look Quickly

Doing 70 on 95
The sanitized,
Transistorized,
Air-conditioned Pass fast judgment
On the poor bastards
In the '44 Berlin-
Looking world
of temporary dreams
and never-ending
nightmares.

The countless gutted
gutter-snipes,
souls as
abandoned as
the buildings,
minds
burned out by
the arsonists
on street corners
and in treeless parks,
take little notice
of their judges.

The condemners stare
as the smoke rises,
and the sirens
blare the anthem
of the streets above.

LOUIS ROMANO

They point their
all-knowing fingers
as if at the zoo, and change the subject
quickly if their children
ask if people
really live up there.

June 21, 1978

To Freddy

He never met
a German who
loved a Jew.

And I never
met a deli
man who fell

for a philosopher.

March 25, 1982

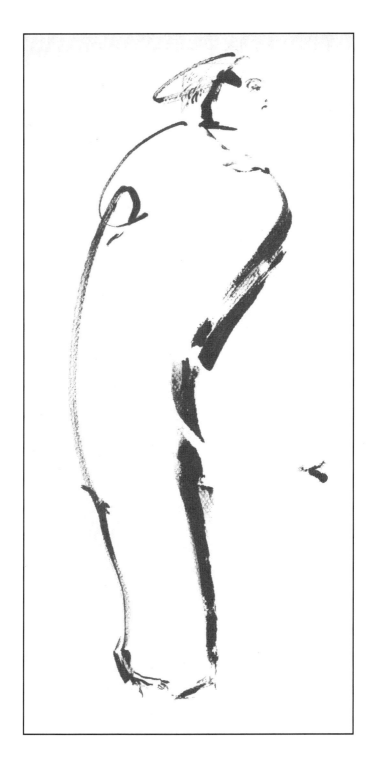

Thoughtrise

For the first time
I waited for the sun
To rise.
My jaw hurt from the sleep missed
And numbness was
The only sensation.
Chirping birds,
An occasional
passing car,
but mostly thoughts
on what
this day would
unfold, thoughts
on thoughts upon
more thoughts,
visions of waiting
for another sun
with another sore jaw
and thoughts.

April 14, 1977

Tunnel Vision

With crust as thick
as their evening
tongues,
glaring
down and quickly
away
for fear their
eyes
will tarnish
the famed spoon

One mustn't stare
at the man
in the wheelchair

unless the chair
is at the summer
cottage on the Cape,

God help them
if they ever
have to bang for
steam.

March 1983

LOUIS ROMANO

LOUIS ROMANO

Puke

The rowboat's sickening
Movements begin;
Stomachs heave and contract
Spitting up their rank remains.
Heads pound like the beating
Of a Latin drum.
Eyes bulge.
Noses run Ears ring.
Teeth chatter.
Lips shiver.
Many colors appear,
Disappear,
Appear again.
The rowboat's sickening
Movements end.

Why did we sell ourselves
For a Dramamine pill?

April 28, 1977

LOUIS ROMANO

Trivia Kings

The details of life
Excite those
Who are overcome
By the enormity
Of real living.

California

December 12, 1978

LOUIS ROMANO

LOUIS ROMANO

Walk...Don't Run

Crunching leaves
Underfoot,
Passing piles
Of passed-away flowers
Giving thought only to
The pigeon path
Laid out
By other dreamers,
Those other runners
Who never stopped
To notice
Why the flowers died,
And never
Laid their own paths.

June 9, 1978

2076 Revisited

I made a left
And found myself
In my old world.
Destroyed as it is,
Departed from reality,
As it once was
Upon a better time,
And nothing but
A few remnants
Cried out
For eyes
That have known them.
And these eyes
Wept dry tears
For the
Memories.

April 11, 1977

LOUIS ROMANO

Augie

The old fellow
saw spies in his
mirror.
He wanted someone
to chase the spies
but not damage the
mirror, which was old, too.
He put his hat
on one morning
and left to
check-in
to report about
those spies,
never to return,
He joined the
spies, always
watching those
who were left,
and waiting
until they too
could see all the spies.

May 21, 1978

C

The big
C is gonna
Getcha baby
S'gonna getcha
Soon. Sooner'n
You think, y'all.
And when it
Grabs yo ass,
It don let go.
Try n put
Some shit in yo
Veins, but ain't
No use...you gonna
Die cause the big C's
Done gottcha baby.
It done gottcha bad.
Jes hope n' pray
You go fast
An don't forget
To say yo
Goodbyes babys.
Before you say
Yo prayers.

April 13, 1978

LOUIS ROMANO

For Marty

The sun
reflected off the
concrete, squeezing
my eyes closed.
The cracks in the
slabs were
the only road signs
back to the house.
The nickel pickle
exploded in my
mouth and let
me remember it
a good while.
The neighborhood
Was beautifully
noisy:
baby carriages squeaked,
a bus passed a block away.
Opera from the
fourth floor window.
A scooter, a little girl
Playing A my name is
Anna and my husband's
Name is Angelo we
Came from Alaska and
We sell apples
A car's screeching wheels
Stop everything
An eerie silence
Takes over for a

Few seconds.
The sounds begin
One at a time
And build back
To normal.
car missed
A cat.
I was sitting
On the stoop.
Letting the
Afternoon pass,
a little bored,
worried
about starting
Fourth grade in two weeks.
Butterflies flew
In my stomach
as I thought about the
nun who might be
my new teacher.
Mom said:
"Be a good boy, Louis,
And maybe Sunday,
Mutt will take you
To the country"
My senses soared
Past the rooftops
Over the kites.
I could see the
Neighborhood from
All sorts of different

LOUIS ROMANO

Angles.
Mutt! He took me
Downtown last summer.
Now the country!
Unbelievable!
Years passed
And I got
A little jealous
When I saw Mutt
Taking some kids
Off to some
Exotic place.
The zoo, a museum
Maybe a movie.
He was a great teacher. His subjects were
sharing, generosity, caring, and
His pupils all passed
With flying colors.
He taught them well.

August 21, 1981

LOUIS ROMANO

Fire Flies

Thousands of fireflies
Illuminate the park,
Like so many twinkling stars.

They cast a moment of light,
That's missed if you blinked your eyes.
Their lives are short, but their jobs aren't.
They fly around, ever twinkling, always twinkling.
They have purpose, direction.
There is a goal to their lives.
The twinkling has a reason.
The reason is clear.
They are gifts from nature,
To bring smiles to our lips and
To make life a bit brighter.

July 14, 1974

The Swagger

He walked up to the
Kids playing stickball
With the stroll he had always had
Approaching the chalk plate
Chewing bubble gum and wearing sneakers.
They sensed his greatness,
But doubted his ability.
He knew how great he was
Before his belly fell over his belt.
He asked the kid for a swing.
He took the stick and ball,
looked straight down the street
Four sewers was the best
he'd settle for.
The ball bounced once, twice,
the mighty swing met the
rubber ball:
a short grounder
was the result.
Embarrassed
he threw the kid a quarter
and walked away.
"Hey mister, that ball's sixty cents."
He turned, threw his gum to the kid:
"Keep the change."

September 16, 1977

The Stickball King

He still walks
With his sense
Of nobility, through
His kingdom of asphalt
And concrete.
He stops at a manhole cover
And remembers how
He would hit the pink ball
Past four maybe five
Of them with a style
All his own.
The chalk markings
Were his record of victories,
The battles of the streets.

And, after a decade
Of brutal matches
The king of broomsticks
And black tape
Has his indelible memories.
Unlike the chalk scoreboard,
They will never
wash away.

September 26, 1978

The Street Corner

I've been on this corner
For thirty years;
God things have changed.
It seems
Like only yesterday
That Rock 'n' Roll music
Was here
With boys and girls
Who would hang out
All dressed up funny
Chewing the penny gum
They bought from me;
Once in a while
They bought a coke,
A lime ricky or an egg cream,
But I remember
Always chasing then away
When they got too loud,
You know
That crazy music
And all.

LOUIS ROMANO

LOUIS ROMANO

Hopscotch

Jumping From
Lover
      To
            Lover
      To
Lover
Picking up the
Wasteland
Memories.
Doing the
Eight boxes.
If you step on
A line,
Nobody's back is broken.
You simply start
Again,
Being more
Careful at
Every start.

January 22, 1978

The Reservation

Life is no joking matter.
It's not too serious either.
Somewhere between
laughter and tears
is the promised land.
You can see it any time you wish
In the eyes of babies
And in the silence of the dead.

Innocence or experience
Are one in the same.
Innocence limits what you can do.
Experience limits what you will do.
And the promised land is still
Reserved for the chosen few.

August 14, 1973

Half Is Nothing

On one of those dreary
Days,
I searched back into my
Mind's file.
For happier times.
I went through years in seconds, like a Nova
And pulled out all the
Regrets, mistakes,
Embarrassments, sorrows.
And erased all the could-haves.
I was left with all the good
Thoughts of how life has treated me.
Nothing but happiness.
I then realized that without
These hurdles in my life
It would have been too easy.
So I quickly updated
My file, and the sun
Came out.

April 27, 1977

LOUIS ROMANO

Seizure

From behind
It grasped my hand
And lifted it
Towards the sky,
Then back towards itself.
Turning slightly
Expecting to see
Something familiar
I saw nothing.
My head could not
Return to its place,
As if caught
In a painless vise.
A strange hum
Engulfed me.
My senses no longer
Under my control,
I gave up looking
For the familiar
And turned to memory
For refuge.
No consolation.
No comparison.
No history.
No help.
I was totally controlled.
Totally!

LOUIS ROMANO

Since then,
Without showing,
For fear it will
Return,
I worship every moment
Of freedom.

April 13, 1978

LOUIS ROMANO

LOUIS ROMANO

.

Man Plans

I am the pilot of a craft,
Taking off to nowhere.
I am an admiral of a ship
That is sinking, gradually.
I am a champion,
Who has been defeated.

I laugh in the face of adversity
Then cry before my mirror.
There is no truer judge of me,
Than me.

I am a pilot of a craft,
Flying.
I am an admiral of a ship
Which rules the sea.
I am an undefeated champion.

The answer, is not difficult at all.
I will be whatever I want to.
Champion or failure. Failure or Champion.
It's all my doing.

Unless God has a say.

LOUIS ROMANO

Lighten Up!

Hard words
Hard looks
Harsh feelings,
But deep down
You want to
Throw your
Head back
And enjoy
Me.

Soft words
Softer looks
Easy feelings
But deep down
You want
To throw your
Head back
And ignore
Me.

February 19, 1978

LOUIS ROMANO

Parasites

The self-important
Green between
The teeth,
Mucus-snorting
Slobs.
Emitting their
Foul-smelling
Punk-rocking
Breath.
Into the same
Air that
Decent folk
Breathe.
Force-feeding
Their pukey
Green bile
Of a smile on those poor, unknowing folk…
Like the beautiful sweetness
Of the Venus plant
Before the crushing
Leaves suck out
The very life of
The noble folk.

December 28, 1979

LOUIS ROMANO

Ill-usions

Rooms designed
in earth tones,
long, polished bars
that have no odor
(as bars should have),
antiseptic toilets, clean sheets,
so many sirs, yes sirs,
thank you sirs,
anonymous faces,
that have taken
anonymous roads,
all with un-beveled
mirrors that create
ill-usions
in simpler days.
There were much simpler
fantasies in those days.

September 30, 1977 (Seattle, Washington)

Butterflies

Stomach butterflies
fluttered until
the first opponent
was faced.
And each of the
nine gladiators,
In their own way,
deeply inside
would recall
the gladiators
phrase.
"Hail Caesar
we, who are
about to die,
salute you."
Then the first pitch
came in and the
butterflies scattered.

May 31, 1978

The Turnstile

The waiting room
Could have a turnstile.
Just for a count.
No age, religion, sex,
Size, nationality.

Just the turnstile will do.
Names on walls—the singer,
The writer, the madame,
a group of others—
Points to the charity
Of the place.

Engulfed in hope…
The clock still runs
Not missing a
Darned tick.

Looming over the room
Is an incessant aura,
A dense cloud
Trying to be a memory
By science, prayers, voodoo.
Name it!

And the ticking of the clock
Is starting to sound like
A turnstile.

Too Much Tube?

Turn to the Tube.
That great and powerful
Glass eye.
Only once a year do we get to see:
The drama of Jerry Lewis
The stupidity of the Emmys
The boobs of the Oscars
The Stupid Bowl–Half time's always a hoot.
The mistakes of the Union. What smiles…what hair
What Drivel!
And of course,
The *Wizard of Oz* with 70 commercials.
That tube…
Man…it started out with real wonder,
but it got into the wrong hands.
Like a dirty bomb.
When they realized that it could
Mesmerize
The Uncle Miltyesque had no chance
But to watch along
With
The rest of us.

December 2006

LOUIS ROMANO

The Shut-in

4 deadbolt locks
a peep hole, three chains,
a Medco police lock
bolted into the black tile floor.
Bars on every window,
both of them.
She never left the flat
except to shop
for a few things to eat,
and these trips were rare.

The Andrea TV hadn't
worked in years.
A telephone wasn't needed.
Once there was one, but it
stopped ringing in 1972.
Her mailbox was smashed and her
check was stolen weeks ago.

She sits
in a sheet-draped, worn-out,
spring-less, lifeless, armless
old chair rereading a
42-year-old love letter
with a box of graying
photographs on her lap
so if she were to die suddenly
she wouldn't be
alone.

February 18, 1978

LOUIS ROMANO

When Life Is A Ledger

Debit this credit that,
credit this debit that.
An accountant he had
25 years of loyal service.
Undying loyal service.
8:10 train in by 5 of 9.
Coffee apple Danish.
Work work work work
Credit debit debit credit
10:00 break. Read paper.
10:10 work work work
Credit debit
12 lunch.
Brown bag, one sandwich, 1 cookie.
glass of milk.
12:30 work work debit credit.
5 of 5 clear desk sharpen pencils
5 out
5:20 train 6:15 home.
One scotch, some dinner.
9:30 bed.
And so it went for those many years.
One day,
8:10 train in by 5 of 9
coffee, apple Danish
work work debit…
pink envelope on desk.

.

"Due to bla bla bla your position has
been terminated bla bla bla, in 2 weeks,"...
credit.
10:00 break. Read paper.
12:00 lunch
brown bag 1 sandwich, 1 cookie,
glass of milk.
12:30 work work work debit credit
5 of 5 clear desk, sharpen pencils
5 out.
"Ladies and gentleman due to blah blah blah
beyond our control the 5:20 train
has been
delayed."

LOUIS ROMANO

The Gift From God

When I thought
I had seen
Most of the beautiful things,
The shockingly beautiful things
In this world
And thought there
Would be nothing more
I looked in a direction
Only fate could
Direct me
And was gifted
Truly gifted
With an
Eyegasm
At the sight
Of
You.

July 1977

LOUIS ROMANO

Card Collection

The cards are piling up
Sometimes two in a week
With that beautiful
Laminated sheen
And stunning backlit sky
With small colorful birds.
And yellow or gold circles
Around the heads of the robed ones.
The cards are piling up
They are.
Enough to cover the mirror
With the words o gentlest heart,
O merciful savior… grant us…
Bla bla bla
Not so scary anymore
As it once was.
This collection
Ends
With mine
Unseen.

June 2007

LOUIS ROMANO

Dear Judy Lee

With your southern
Ways and manners,
With your soft whisper
Voice and that easy drawl,
You look and sound so good

Surely men will think of you
As solid sugar.
Sweet as can be.

How special you are.

I, my dear, also feel you
Are sugar.

To an open cavity

Shooting pain
Straight to my brain.

May 21, 1978

A Story

So she cried
The first time
He said he loved her.

Not a whimper, not a torrent
But a soft cry
With a few tears. Nice. Lovely
(she was brought up not to cry you know).

She needed very much
To hear those words.

To
        Feel those words,
        Touch those words,
        Sense those words,
        Taste those words,
Again.

So she cried.

And with time, a very short time
Those words escaped
Their meaning.

And stuff, the stuff of life
And its complications and
Silly situations
Got in the way.

And the applause of love
Was silenced so abruptly
That maybe those words...

Were...
Only
Words.

But just what if?

July 2007

LOUIS ROMANO

Are We Having Fun Yet?

You have spoken like a true Zionist bastard. Not that you are a
bastard or a Zionist but you just sound like one sometimes. Or
is that a Muslim fundamentalist or a Born-Again Christian on a
rampage?

We must categorize each other or we are not having any fun…
right? I on the other hand could be referred to as a fallen-away
papist, a radical anti-Catholic buffoon who was mentally brutalized
by lesbian nuns and pedophile priests and brothers more afraid
of dying and their own sexuality than I am of pit bulls on a flimsy
rope held by a black man who was brutalized by whites in Macon,
Georgia on a hot night in 1967.

Don't you see my point darlings? It's senseless. All of it. Fighting
and hatred is a waste of energy and brain cells that can be used for
the good of our time on this earth. Amen, amen, and amen again.
Now, if I ever again use the N-word, my dick should turn green and
wilt like a fifteen-day-old cut flower.

But not a carnation please. We don't like carnations now, do we?

There you go, separating the flowers, having our favorites. Flower
Prejudice. The carnations will forever more be deemed less than
other flowers. This could be another cause. Just think of the endless
hatefulness that can grow from this. Carnations must be separated
from the roses and other plants of noble birth. They cannot be given
water from the same vessels as the other flowers. When they are
delivered, they need to be in the back of the van. Better yet, they

should not be in the same vehicle. Better yet, let's see that they are not even in the same vase as the other flowers. How dare they contaminate the good flowers? It's time that we stand together and fight for what's right. Once and for all!

Testa di Sciccu

The donkey
Knows only what he needs,
But he is ordered to do what
Others want.
So he gets pushed and
Whipped until
One day
He tells himself
(in donkey talk)
Fuck this shit.
And walks off into the mountains
Where he finds
That he gets what he needs.
Easy.

LOUIS ROMANO

Finally

For what seems like
My whole life
Looking around every corner,
Under every rock,
In every place that I've been.
I called for your touch
In the very early morning hours
And pined for your presence.
You don't even know
How cruel my not knowing you
Has been.
But I'll search on
Until I find you…
Then forgive you
For not allowing me
To find you sooner.

December 1977

LOUIS ROMANO

Waiting In The Doctor's Office

She sat in her chair.

You know, the kind that has wheels.
And air to breathe through plastic tubes.

She waging war within her body.
He stalwart, showing strength for her.

She a bit twisted, a bit slumped to one side.
Nodding out from moment to moment.
Holding her man in a cramped hand.

He with a smile and look that said every moment was important.

Looking lovingly into each other's eyes and beyond.

Into each other's souls.

Both not betraying their losses.

Not knowing,

What could have been.

Not knowing,
What will presently be.

They will be again soon enough.
Holding hands, running on a beach.

December 2010

Acknowledgements

Without the professional art direction of Anita Sancinella this book would simply be a pamphlet. Many thanks to Mary Lynn Romano for proof reading and editing so if there are mistakes please contact her.

I especially want to thank Alexa Guariglia for allowing me to include her abundant artistic talents in this book.

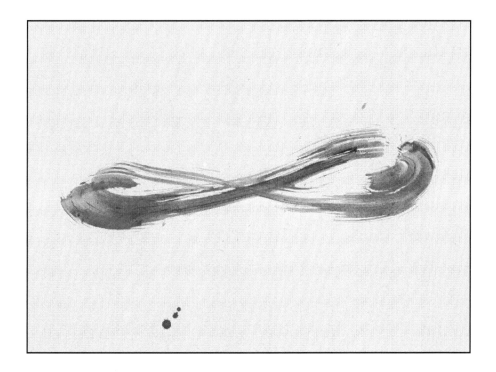

Made in the USA
Charleston, SC
26 May 2011